I0766700

Created Equal

Do you love God or money?
Well? Let's fix things now.

Ben Fournier

Copyright © 2019 Ben Fournier

All rights reserved.

DEDICATION

To all the crappy employers, who showed me what life is like for most people, who live struggling from paycheck to paycheck, barely surviving.

ACKNOWLEDGMENTS

Thank you to my few true friends and everyone who has been supportive of my attempts at being an author even if it isn't a "real job", whatever the heck that's supposed to be. It seems to me no matter how much anyone earns, unless their income exceeds the GDP of the planet it apparently isn't good enough, so why should anyone care to meet impossible standards and worry so much about tomorrow and what each day may bring?

"Now listen, you rich people! Cry and moan over the miseries that are overtaking you. Your riches are rotten, your clothes have been eaten by moths, your gold and silver are corroded, and their corrosion will be used as evidence against you and will eat your flesh like fire. You have stored up treasures in these last days. Look! The wages that you kept back from the workers who harvested your fields are shouting out against you, and the cries of the reapers have reached the ears of the Lord of the Heavenly Armies."

-James 5:1-4

DEMAND BASED PRICING AND WAGES ARE ABSURD

Does a single bedroom broken down house deserve a price tag in the millions of dollars? No. Not even if it's in a famous city. Junk is junk and shouldn't cost absurd prices. But of course, "supply and demand!" chant it, because that's apparently all that matters even though it leads to absurd situations. It needs to be limited to reasonable levels. A house in a famous city, especially when just a pile of mold and raccoon dung, shouldn't be priced as much as a castle in good repair. It just shouldn't. Can you see this? And if the result of demand based pricing leads to wrong situations, then obviously it is the wrong method to be used.

Quite the same with wages. Does anyone earn 10 million per year? Can anyone? Absolutely not. Sitting on one's butt and making a few basic decisions does not earn such absurd wages, not in the least. And "unskilled workers" killing themselves, being forced by employers under extortionary threats of losing what little livelihood they have if they don't work any hours scheduled.

Oh, but that's just how things are done, and if it's the way they're done then that makes it "okay", right? No. I know, in economics textbooks, they have formulas for adjusting only the wages of workers, philosophies of investors and owners first, and other forms of stacking the deck for themselves. That is wrong, though I may never be able to prove it to those which are convinced that extreme capitalism is the one true religion. It's intuitively obvious regardless.

Sure, investors should get their money back, perhaps with simple interest and maybe no more than double their principle. If the borrower can't pay it back, just heaping on more debt that they can't pay is not going to "benefit the economy", it will lead most to just give up caring because living has been made impossible under the crushing debt.

Speaking of crushing debt, colleges are absurdly priced too. When I went to college for accounting, it was $2,000 per class for most classes and I had to do 3 or 4 classes per quarter in order to get the stupid financial aid. I never wanted to go to college, my thoughts were along the line's of Will Hunting's in the movie Good Will Hunting for many years before starting, but it was one of the requirements my now ex-wife had for me before she'd consider marrying me. It's absurd in every respect. Often the textbooks are cheap yet overpriced garbage, and always in new editions so as to make sure you can't sell them back for anywhere near the price you paid. But, it does allow you to buy the textbooks at used book stores for cheap at least, so you can study college textbooks for $7 to $22 dollars about rather than thousands of dollars in student loans.

So what should be done? Ah, the joy of proposing solutions to be shot down. Basically, set maximum wages and maximum prices for the basics of food, shelter, and utilities. Nobody earns millions yearly, that money is stolen from the workers. Perhaps a maximum wage of no more than $111,000 yearly should work. Maximum prices for basics should be a percentage of the lowest wage workers. Luxury items can be priced whatever businesses want, and fast food should be considered a luxury while food from grocery stores are mostly basics.

Oh, but so many members of upper management are oh so highly "skilled" ... at making simple decisions and doing formal meetings, hobnobbing with other overpaid rich brats, and so much wasteful nonsense otherwise. Yeah, how about no? Really almost anyone could do what they do, with minimal training. Probably less training than is required to "flip burgers" and all the other tasks and psychological abuse at fast food workplaces. What little actual work they do isn't worth how much they pay themselves at the cost of the workers underneath them.

Heck, probably they could all be replaced with a single virtual intelligence, not that you'd really want amoral computers heartlessly running things, but heartless and immoral humans are just about as bad in practice at times.

They steal from their workers and threaten to replace them with mechanical robots, while all the lazy overpaid seat warmers which steal from their workers legalistically could be replaced with software that doesn't require mechanics to constantly fix as robots at factories do every few minutes when out of calibration or encountering unforeseen circumstances.

Sure, there can be unforeseen circumstances which human leadership might be better for, but hey, as long as they excuse underpaying their workers with using robots as an excuse then their pay should be cut under excuse of replacing them with mere software. They can figure out how to survive off of all their "golden handshakes" and sell a few of their yachts and summer homes.

College prices also need to decrease, but the way to do that is by removing student loans. Have only grants at their current levels and no more loans, and do not allow colleges to issue their own loans either. Their prices are artificial and will drop like a rock into Jupiter once they're no longer thrown money at.

That's exactly what's happening too, they are being thrown money at, by the state, and what the state is buying are debt slaves. Deliberately. That is probably the entire purpose of making student loans an indelible debt.

Also, what is with states stealing away certifications and driver's licenses from people who can't afford their student loans? That's entirely counterproductive, if they want their money paid back. But they don't. They want people to become dependent on the state. Oh, but aren't I arguing for communism just because I'm criticism the way things are with darwinian capitalism? Why? Why does it have to be either absurd extreme? Both only benefit the oligarchs. Yes, both.

You want to just say "look what this tyranny did! Let's blame the economic system!", but every government has always been oligarchy, rule by the rich, the few fortunate thieves which steal from the poor.

In America, we have two types of oligarch essentially, harvesters and collectors. The harvesters are the ones hiding behind the guise of capitalism to steal as much as possible from the artificially impoverished, they own the businesses and funnel most of the funds upwards to themselves.

The collectors are of course the thieves in public control of the state, the ones usually thought of in the trite yet true phrase of "taxation is theft". Really both forms are theft, both taxation and extortionary unilateral contracts.

There should be limits placed upon both Caesars as to how much we are required to render to these thieves. Neither form of oligarch deserve to steal so much away, to live in palaces while the poor are nearly homeless.

So, set limits: put politicians on minimum wage and freeze their rich assets while they're in office, to let them understand what it's like to be poor; set maximum wages for owners of megacorporations and all the absurd levels of middle and upper management and everyone else who is overpaid.

Small businesses likely won't have owners overpaying themselves as much, and perhaps for them they can pay minimum wage, but for the megacorporations they should pay at least living wages as their minimum wage, thus bypassing all the nonsense about living wage laws destroying small businesses.

It would only harm the larger businesses and allow the smaller businesses a chance to compete with practical monopolies like WallFart and the various other giants that step on the little guy. Small businesses should only be consisting of a single building in a single location, not be a giant business posing as a small business.

Really minimum wage should be a living wage, but for the sake of getting past the "oh small businesses will die" argument, let the actually small businesses have an exception for them. Hopefully by putting better limits on the prices of food, shelter, and utilities ought to make such things more affordable, and setting maximum wages (rather than the current system of letting harvester-oligarchs use extortionary contracts to gather most of the wealth, that is then collected by their buddies in the state) ought to allow for more money to be paid for the workers and/or used to grow the business and allow for more workers.

Oligarchs which still violate maximum wage laws via creative accounting or whatever other method ought to be put in prison. Regular prison at that and not palace prisons for "white collar criminals". They're all criminals, so put them all together. Oh, but they'll move to a better country. Okay, then, they can join their comrades in other nations where their wage slaves mostly are. Maybe they can find work there too, enjoy that "good honest hard work" they love putting so many through.

What about health care? Cut the prices down there, too, they're insane. Declare a year of jubilee already for all the debt by which they justify crazy prices. Should healthcare be a public service rather than a luxury? Yes, it should. Oh, but what about bloated bureaucracies which make for absurd waiting times? Get rid of bureaucracies then, they're the real problem for timing issues. There should be a right to life and health for everyone, both born and unborn. We're all created equal in the image of God, so both rich and poor deserve to live and not be murdered by either action or inaction regardless of justifications of worshiping money or convenience or anything else.

For mothers which don't want their babies, adoption should be freely available. Not abortion or any other form of infanticide, but adoption. The would-be murdered babies should instead go to families which will properly love and care for them. As for previous doctors which have committed murder, they should be dealt with as murderers and face capital punishment. "Back alley abortionists" should be actively sought out and dealt with likewise. We're all made in the image of God and those which shed human blood, they are murderers. Same with euthanasia and convincing the infirm to give up on life, such eugenicists ought to be dealt with as murderers if they have ended human life.

My own nation of America has murdered tens of millions of babies, thanks to the religion of hedonism and the pervasive eugenics propaganda spread throughout media and the state controlled education system. How long will this go on until America, and the other nations which murder babies and starve the poor, are judged by God? It can't go on too much longer. God may be slow to anger, but how many generations of tempting His wrath do you want to give Him? It would be best to repent. Nothing can be done to get back the lives of the murdered, but the murders should cease ASAP.

Regardless of however much we're paid or pay ourselves at the cost of others, born or unborn, young or old, we're all made in the image of God and that is how we are created equal. Murdering or shortening the lifespans of fellow human beings is wrong. There should be no struggle for mere basics. The ends do not justify the means though, and even if my suggestions are imperfect something should still be done to make it work, but make it work rightly. Both the ends and the means must be good, or else the result is wrong. "The way we win matters" as the character Ender Wiggin said, and so

make both the ends and the means good and not just
one or the other.

FREEDOM OF SPEECH AND COGNITIVE FUNCTIONS

I see all the whining about "hate speech" and other doubleunplus good words as a matter of people valuing social harmony over authenticity. Basically Fe, extraverted feeling, is being treated as superior to Fi, introverted feeling. Fe is basically socially harmony and going along with group values, while Fi is valuing authenticity and individual morals.

Should it be this way? No. Authenticity is better than fake niceness, quite obviously. Having the state and businesses violate freedom of speech for the sake of forced niceness is immoral.

Oh, but of course, there are legalistic loopholes which allow businesses to violate all the natural rights of everyone. But should they? No. Both the state and the businesses are the government, whether in private or public office, oligarchs are the actual rulers and they should not have rights superseding the rights of individuals.

Similarly freedom of the press should not be limited to only state licensed media outlets, but everyone should be free to say whatever they like. The owners of websites should not be permitted to violate the freedom of speech of the users, and neither words nor thoughts be confused as actions in a court of law or drumhead otherwise.

Social media should be considered the press, since for the majority of the population it is our press, yet the rich owners of everything control what little free speech we have by shadow banning, blocking, deleting, etc. Such are freedom of speech violations, regardless of how it's legalistically "okay" in the eyes of the flaw, but such violations should be made illegal.

But yeah, it might hurt feelings if people say things. Yes, I'm sure it will, but are feelings more important than freedom? No. For as nice as social harmony may seem from the outside, such is essentially a fakeness that cannot last. It is better to be real, to be authentic and let people say what they mean and be corrected as necessary with words.

Notice that: with words. Not with fines. Not with imprisonment. Not with stealing away one's livelihood. Just with words. Words for words. Let people argue, respectfully preferably but even disrespectful argumentation is superior to artificially enforced social harmony.

Oh, but what if racists say racist things? So what? They will anyway. It doesn't combat such superficial prejudice to violate their freedom of speech. If anything, going by Morgan Freeman's notion of essentially ignoring irrelevant differences ought to work. Think of the 80's, the television and movies then. Sure, you have tropes, but how many characters made irrelevant issues about skin color? Almost none. I don't remember any, but I'm sure there probably were, but either way you just have to not care. People imitate each other, and if such stupid irrelevant matters as the melanin percentage on the skin are ignored, then most will ignore it.

However, nonsense like pretending people are racist because they don't have darker skin serves only to perpetuate racism, since reverse racism is racism. Baiting as well. But should either form of racism be censored for the sake of social harmony? No. Each person, individually has to ignore the nonsense and not fund the oligarchs which keep trying to drag it out. Let the actual racists be authentic, but ignore them and don't let them control you.

I think freedom of speech should be absolute, for speech. Words and actions are two separate things. There should be no control over the words of people, regardless of ownership or wealth or whatever excuse.

It's funny how so often people will just point to arbitrary rules in terms of service by which oligarchs grant themselves the ability to violate rights, and so many people saying "the first amendment doesn't really mean anything" basically.

Firstly, freedom of speech is a natural right, and not given by the state, so it's not just for Americans or anyone in particular nor should it be violated for anyone.

Secondly, who cares how it's subverted or limited? It shouldn't be. Just because the oligarchs in power over everything legalistically can do whatever they want, that doesn't make it right. Just because the private-rich grease the pockets of the state-rich and can do anything, that doesn't make it right.

Like how apartments which are homes pretend the owners of the building hold the 4th amendment rights and workplaces are free to violate the second amendment, that doesn't make it right for them to do so.

Remember this quote: "I wholly disapprove of what you say and will defend to the death your right to say it." And I don't care who said it, whether it was said by Voltaire or anyone else, it matters not. The idea behind it still stands. This is how people should behave, allowing others to speak regardless of disagreement, rather than going "heretic!" and silencing their opposition legalistically according to the corrupt laws of the state.

Generally, the more freedom the better, even if it is disharmonious. But speaking of which, let's go onto the next point about rights.

THE RIGHT TO SELF DEFENSE

As the maxim goes, "an armed society is a polite society", so for those which value enforcing social harmony they really ought to want the natural right to bear arms to be permitted generally. But often not so much, mainly due to how the oligarchs have the artificial divide of political parties (both of which are the same, but just use different rhetoric to appeal to different types) such that the platform which appeals most to high Fe types also associates with disarming the people, and high Fe types go with the group values above their own.

Oh, but what about firearm deaths, accidents and so many Operation Northwoods style shootings that happened since Mary's Lamb was no longer allowed in schools? All the deaths that happened due to teaching children we're just animals and indoctrinating them into atheism en masse? Isn't that due to guns? Because guns are violent all by themselves apparently and teaching children to be hedonistic sociopaths has nothing to do with it. No. Might as well ban cars too, there are tons of accidents and buying gasoline sends money to nations which murder civilians for things the left supports.

But what limits should there be on civilian weaponry? I don't, but for now I'll say anything short of nukes. Really nations shouldn't have nukes either. I mean, seriously, always being ready to incinerate most cities and poison all life on the surface of Earth in a single hour? What the heck? That needs to stop. Nuclear weapons should be dismantled and turned into engines for interplanetary spacecraft instead.

Civilians in that case would be handling such materials I suppose, but I'm sure there's a good and right way to do such things.

There should probably be more focus on making life more bearable for everyone in general rather than protecting everyone from themselves and presuming everyone is a criminal and act like they're guilty until proven ever more guilty. The more that people are treated like criminals, the more they will act like criminals. And vice versa. Most people just want to have a happy life, though some do bad things, regardless of whether they are civilians or police or soldiers. Good and bad exist within each group, and removing the ability of one group to protect themselves will only make it so the bad members of each group have the advantage.

Removing the rights of the lawful good doesn't protect them or anyone else from those which are evil, whether the evil are lawful evil, neutral evil, or chaotic evil. The lawful evil will likely only go after those which they have a melee advantage over, or harm others legalistically at least; the neutral and chaotic evil won't care to follow the laws and like with cities having strict gun laws the criminals will still have guns while the lawful good are defense-less. So the right to carry armaments should not be infringed.

HOMES ARE HOMES REGARDLESS OF THE PROPERTY OWNER AND INTERNAL ESPIONAGE

Basically, as the title says, such is my interpretation of the natural rights affirmed by the 4th amendment. What do I mean by that though?

Say you're living in an apartment. They suck don't they? Always having neighbors running above you, music playing too loud, and you don't even have a lawn of your own to yell at people to get off of. But what's even worse is having no right to deny entry to the henchmen of the ubermafia. The 4th amendment rights rest in the laps of the owners, and so they can invite themselves in whenever they want and let police enter and do anything too.

Letter of the law versus spirit of the law

though, such is an immoral situation. Your home is your home, regardless of paperwork. Such behavior should be considered home invasion on the part of the people paid often absurd costs to wave rules around and generally ignore repairs that need to be made until after you leave so they can pretend you never mentioned them and keep your deposit.

And the various nonsense of being spied on through everything for the sake of valuing safety over liberty, oh give me a break. The power and control freaks and all their gestapo clone agencies need to be defunded and removed. Spend the money wasted on treating everyone on the planet as a criminal instead on feeding the poor. Really, with 50 billion land animals fed plants and slaughtered each year, if removing animals from that you could feed tens of billions more humans just with current surface area usage. Having food is a basic need, and such should be done for those unable to feed themselves for the moment, while helping them develop everything they need to be independent. Instead of treating everyone like criminals, instead care for their basic needs and let them be grateful to you.

The Department of War itself takes in hundreds of billions of dollars and spends ever more. Cut down their funding, merge the departments into the National Guard and Coast Guard, and only defend our own borders rather than police the world anymore. The less we make enemies of everyone, the less we'll have enemies to fight.

Sure, some have philosophies of belligerence,

but treat each person individually and investigate them only when there really is probable cause enough to warrant investigation. Each person in the world has a chance to be saved, to accept Jesus is Lord and no longer follow the paths of their parents. So demonizing anyone is essentially counterproductive to evangelism – which should be the ultimate goal, bringing people to Christ, and not just having hegemonic control over the world for mere avarice.

Do you love God or money?

ONE NATION UNDER GOD

Secularism should never have been included in the Constitution. It should be that America, and the rest of the nations really, should be nations which acknowledge the God of the Bible and not allow for atheists and other religions to run amok. No one brand of churchianity ought to be counted as the Church though, since the Church is composed of every true believer in Christ regardless of the brand they associate with. The state also should not be counted as superior to the Church either, but Christian morality, based in the Bible, is what ought to be legislated rather than the amorality of atheism and so much "brave new world" nonsense.

Making it Christian from the outset could have prevented the mass shootings in schools and so many other crimes also. Instead, we have the religious philosophy of atheism taught as truth from the state indoctrination factories which barely even teach basic grammar anymore and continue to shift from academics to churning out social justice warriors for the state which chant "take our rights away for peace and safety!"

Yeah, sure, we've all been indoctrinated to automatically think the suggestion of having a Christian nation be considered "evil", but guess who has done that indoctrination? The state, and the father of lies behind the state.

Oh, but of course there were Christian nations in the past which did bad things, and by necessity such has to be repeated. Right? No. Separate out the bad, keep the good. That's what needs to be done with anything. Throw out the bathwater, but keep the baby.

STATE CHARITY AND VOLUNTARY TAXATION

Essentially the psittacism for suggesting helping the poor with money from taxation is "oh but that's socialism and socialism is bad! Look what atheistic tyrants in unchecked governments did!" But history need not repeat itself if you learn from it what is necessary to correct it. No more atheism for starters, make the nation a Christian nation and let the saboteurs pretend to be Christians like so many democrat politicians pretend to be republicans. In their social games at least most of their decisions will have to keep Biblical morality in mind, even if they do unfortunately do crap behind the scenes like the US government had done MK Ultra back in the 1950's. Still better that they keep their sin in the dark than prance about in the streets.

But, as for taxation, I say make it voluntary and allow people to designate where it is to be spent. That way people really could vote with their wallets on issues and be able to keep more of their own money rather than be forced under threat of armed robbery and kidnapping to comply with the oli-garchs and their ubermafia.

Sure, many people would stop paying taxes, especially the poor who currently can barely afford surviving. But there are still many people who wor-ship the state and they should pay out of patriot-ism. Heck, maybe they should receive a shiny cer-tificate that they can hang on their wall to show off how patriotic they are.

Churches survive, and thrive even, off of volun-tary payments by their members, and the state can do the same. For a few years, maybe, the state would lose much of its stolen money and have to cut down on things, like perhaps its giant military indus-trial complex and criminal agencies that violate natural rights, but without the theft of the state, the economy would generally improve and more people would be able to donate out of their excess then. Sure, maybe the state wouldn't have so many trillions to waste on killing people and stealing re-sources to make enemies, but internally at least the nation would generally improve.

Then, with voluntary payments, the poor could be assisted in a manner of charity rather than wel-fare with funds from extortion as the current argu-mentation opposed to providing food and shelter for those which can't find work emphasizes.

Make taxation voluntary and it's no longer theft, it's a "patriotic duty" and with about 40% of people being SJ temperament at the very least those will still voluntarily pay, just reward them with fancy papers to decorate their walls and ribbons to wear to show off how good a citizen they are officially, SJ types love that kind of crap, so give them what they like. It's a sale in that sense, but at least the state would be selling rather than stealing anymore.

SWORDS INTO PLOWSHARES

Though this is certainly not the earn the chapter title alludes to, still it's better that things should be done on Earth as it is in Heaven (or new Earth, if different, but IDK.) Anyhow, here are some ideas.

Artillery for fighting forest fires. Basically, instead of regular ordinance you'd have air burst shells that coat the ground below with a fire suppressing substance (like the one gel used in 2011's The Thing, Fire Ice I think, which is supposedly some type of baby powder mixed with water.) Regardless of the exact things used, that's the basic idea. You could have artillery fire in a coordinated fashion to contain and enclosed upon the forest fires and put them out.

Also, you could build walls, like aqueducts, which would have spouts to the side which would be programmed to overflow and make a wall of water and prevent the spread of fire, cordoning off forests into segments rather than letting the fire freely spread as much.

Maybe tanks or APCs could be modified to have

a snowblower attachment, which would hurl dirt up to the top of trees and smother fires without having to bring water in, though of course the tanks would still need fuel. I think it would use less energy to spray dirt that's already there rather than have helicopters dump small quantities of water though.

While under current budget at least, I think funding from the Department of War ought to be spent on at least one orbital ring to jumpstart humanity's colonization of the solar system. The price range for one back in 1982 would have been $77 billion, but in 2017 it's $9 billion. Build as many as we can, at least one, with launch loops, trains to orbit, and shipyards making real ships in orbit, and let's colonize Mars and build centrifugal habitations and so many other wonderful things. These don't have to be pipe dreams, they can be made now, it just seems, instead of such awesomeness, nations apparently value stealing, killing, and destroying as the top priorities rather than making good use of the resources at hand for improving life in general.

Planting fruiting trees along sidewalks and everywhere possible and leaving them accessible to the homeless would help too, at least during harvest season, but the times for ripeness depends on each plant and so they could be planted so more have food for a longer amount of time.

Also, there should be public restrooms with hot water and showers every few miles so as to allow the homeless a place to relieve themselves and keep clean, maybe having a public donation shelf of foodstuffs and clothes, monitored and/or guarded so nobody takes too much, but still let each person take what they need – especially in winter, coats, insulated pants, warm socks, and insulated boots should be put there for certain as the deadly weather approaches in the north.

In the south, where the deadly weather is in the summer, businesses should be required to give at least one bottle or refillable cup of water and not allowed to throw the homeless outdoors when the temperature is above 100 Fahrenheit, unless they're to be brought to another shelter from the deadly heat. Murder can be by either action or inaction, and though inaction would be lesser it still is. Sure, some people are more resourceful than others, but in that state of mind I know I was ready to give up and die most days when I've been homeless. You don't just let people die, or treat them like trash or like robots. They're made in the image of God, just the same as you. You will be held accountable for your actions, regardless of how much irrelevant money and riches you have on Earth.

So, stop making excuses and finding new ways to steal from the poor and stop pretending that they're the real thieves for "mooching" from voluntarily donors when the rich are the real thieves which funnel the earnings of poor up to themselves and keep the poor struggling for survival so they'll be desperate for work just to barely live.

In lieu of proper housing, there should be individual shelters everywhere for the homeless. Perhaps fallout shelters, which could be used as such if ever needed. Yes, hydrogen bombs would nullify their usefulness in cities if hit, but we could increase anti-missile systems and hopefully, if WW3 ever happens, some cities wouldn't be vaporized. Fallout shelters could still be useful then, though they'd still need food and water in them. Maybe have automated hydroponics systems and geothermal generators to power them, and water purification systems. Probably would be easier to build a few large fallout shelters rather than many smaller ones, but the more number of them, with more locations, the more chance for people to survive.

Speaking of geothermal energy, that should really be done way more, especially venting volcanoes before they erupt and harvest the heat and pressure for energy. We have so much molten rock beneath us, so much heat, and it is maintain by exothermic decay and so it is sustainable. So we should build as far down as possible, harvest all that geothermal energy and even control the plasticity of the mantle if coordinated properly, which could reduce earthquakes and prevent life lost by that.

Artificial islands could be built in the pathway of regular hurricanes, covered in vertical style wind mills (the kind that look rather alien, rather than the kind that look like fans,) and that could be used to harvest that wasted energy that otherwise is just a destructive force.

Those constant storms off the coast of South

America, with continuous lightning strikes, a submersible platform should be built, with myriad lightning rods and whatever else is necessary to safely harvest that wasted electricity.

Fossil fuels might run out by the mid 21st century, but gasoline and diesel can be made artificially, though it's inefficient and wasteful, but some could be made for processes and machinery which require it. It would be best to replace gas altogether and no longer buy oil from OPEC nations ahead of time, but if we procrastinate we'll still have to cross that bridge anyhow. Better to start weaning off from the gas before the prices are even more absurd than they've ever been.

It would have been better to have never become virtually dependent on gas anyway, but here we are, but soon we will have to not be and we need to get things in order for still having civilization increase and not let the eugenicists spout their Malthusian excuses for mass murder. They're already preparing people to accept it, with movies like Infinity War and the memes saying "thanos did nothing wrong" which is just absurd. Murder is murder, regardless of whether it's done by individuals or the state.

More food could be grown here on Earth if volume is taken advantage of. Ideas of sky-farming, using skyscrapers have already been made, but there's also growing food underground in hydroponics systems. It's not just surface area, but volume which can be used for growing food. So that increases the maximum population way more.

Still, emigration into space is ideal too. Build orbital rings, and get as many people living throughout the solar system as possible. Earth can grow tons of food in arcologies and whatnot else too, but the more habitations for life made the better. Earth will inevitably become a tyrannical state too, so the more people living out of reach of the tyranny of Earth the better also.

There could be so much done if we just put our minds to it and stop looking for excuses to do nothing. We need to make it so there is life everywhere possible and not procrastinate any more. Enough focus on finding new ways to cause death, but build things to protect life, grow life, and spread life everywhere instead. If we procrastinate until it's too late, the Malthusian lovers of death will have their way and it will be far worse than WW2 or Soylent Green or so many other works of fiction could possibly describe, since the eugenicists have already dehumanized the poor and when given proper excuse it will be a tribulation worse than both the holocaust and holodomor, the rich will still have everything and the poor will be left to die or even killed outright. So many people being convinced by Malthusian propaganda will be the very ones targeted by the oligarchs for elimination, since they will measure the worth of life by their bank accounts alone.

So, yeah, we need to properly utilize the resources here on Earth so there may be far more life than has ever lived before. And we need to become a truly spacefaring civilization and no longer put that off either.

Build at least one orbital ring, mine the moon, colonize Mars and everywhere else possible. So much could have already been done, but hasn't. Still needs to be done and time is running out. It might not be as soon as the 2050s or 2070s, but it will run out eventually if things just remain as they are and nothing new is done in time in sufficient quantities to really improve the situation, and by then it will be too late and the rich will either murder the poor outright or let them starve to death. So it's best to act sooner and preserve as much life as possible.

CHIPS AND IMPLANTS

Time for the X-Files theme song, I know, but seriously do not get chips in your hands. Consider this:

"The second beast forces all people – important and unimportant, rich and poor, free and slaves – to be marked on their right hands or on their foreheads, so that no one may buy or sell unless he has the mark, which is the beast's name or the number of its name."
Revelation 13:16-17

Sure, the chips for financial transactions are just one possible implementation of the mark on the hands, and it sounds like it will be economically coerced across the world. Right now, in Wisconsin and Sweden they are trying out the current iteration of this on a smaller scale, but at some point, when the world is a tyranny, it will be required everywhere on Earth for any official financial transaction.

There's a second type of mark too though, the one on the foreheads. Now, that could just be something as simple as an awkward tattoo, but I doubt it. I think instead that it will be a neural interface, allowing for augmented reality as will as reading thoughts and spying on everyone just like cell-phones are used nowadays.

Basically, though I like futuristic tech in general, it would be a really good idea to avoid and outright refuse this technology for as long as possible.

EXTINCTION LEVEL PHILOSOPHIES

The artificial war between the sexes is just a distraction so as to give the poor someone to blame for the corruption of the state and the unfair circumstances which benefit the oligarchs otherwise.

Both MGTOW and 3rd Wave Feminism are a bunch of horsefeathers. They are both sexism demonizing the other sex, placing the blame upon men or upon women for the actions of the state and the few rich owners of everything. It's neither a patriarchy nor a matriarchy, but an oligarchy that is to blame for the situations faced by most.

The corrupt divorce courts which favor women, does anyone really think the patriarchy would do that? No. Nor have women in general done that either, but a few rich jerks which thereby have financially incentivized divorce and sought to destroy the nuclear family.

Keeping men and women at odds with each other is just another divide and conquer strategy, the same as dividing people into democrats and republicans, which at the politician level it's the same party, but for the people they just sell different rhetoric.

Same with MGTOW and 3rd Wave, both just are yet another distraction game, and so many inequalities are invented by the oligarchs alone. The poor have next to no say over each other, so how could it be that either men should blame women or that women should blame men?

So open your eyes and see you are being taught to blame those innocent of causing the unfair situations both ways. It's not those being crushed under the feet of the rich as they climb their stupid ladders of success ever higher, but the oligarchs instead who are actually in power.

Both men and women should be equal, truly equal and not with either over the other in rights or opportunities. We both have our strengths and weaknesses, and we should work together rather than let the rich set us at odds against each other for their benefit.

Neither are better than the other, but better in different ways. So work within each others strengths rather than forcing or shaming either to do things which are weaknesses for one or the other. Let people do what they want, rather than demanding, oh you must do this or you must do that, but still realize there are differences, both men and women have different limits, and it makes no sense to have people work outside their limits. Such is exploitation, and guess who benefits from exploitation? Is it men in general? Is it women in general? Is it the rich in general? Ding ding ding!

The same ones which pretend it's okay to under-pay their workforce while they drive fancy over-priced cars, have multiple overpriced houses, and so many stupid yachts, they are the ones which set men and women against each other, and while the poor blame the poor, the rich sip their gold foil laced wines out of their solid diamond glasses or whatever the heck wastes of money that they've stolen while everyone is distracted.

FOR DURING THE TRIBULATION

While it may be decades to centuries away, and given how slow progress is centuries seems more likely (at least if my interpretation of Revelation 12:12 were true, though I could be wrong and it could only mean something lame in effect like Plato's statement of "only the dead have seen the end of war" which would rather suck.) Regardless of when it's here, it will be Hell on Earth, far worse than it is now. It will probably be like North Korea all over the world then, with Christians being hunted down like we were during the time of the Early Church back when the Roman Empire made Christianity a capital crime within the evil laws of the state.

So it will suck then, obviously. But what can really be done? Run and hide. And you can hide, though with so many Orwellian measures in place and with whatever the mark will be (my bet are the microchips being tested in Sweden and Wisconsin, once they're required for transactions everywhere) it will be far more difficult to even barely survive, but trust in God. Remember, do not worry:

"No one can serve two masters, because either he will hate one and love the other, or be loyal to one and despise the other. You cannot serve God and riches!

That's why I'm telling you to stop worrying about your life – what you will eat or what you will drink – or about your body – what you will wear.

Life is more than food, isn't it, and the body more than clothing? Look at the birds in the sky. They don't plant or harvest or gather food into barns, and yet your heavenly Father feeds them.

You are more valuable than they are, aren't you? Can any of you add a single hour to the length of your life by worrying? And why do you worry about clothes?

Consider the lilies in the field and how they grow. They don't work or spin yarn, but I tell you that not even Solomon in all his splendor was clothed like one of them.

Now if that is the way God clothes the grass in the field, which is alive today and thrown into an oven tomorrow, won't he clothe you much better – you who have little faith?

So don't ever worry by saying, 'What are we going to eat?' or 'What are we going to drink?' or 'What are we going to wear?' because it is the gentiles who are eager for all those things.

Surely your heavenly Father knows that you need

all of them! But first be concerned about God's kingdom and his righteousness, and all of these things will be provided for you as well.

So never worry about tomorrow, because tomorrow will worry about itself. Each day has enough trouble of its own."

Matthew 6:24-34, ISV

It may be stressful and you may be hiding off the grid and provided for by God like God provided for Elijah by ravens, and maybe some of those who are chipped may still be charitable even though they're rule-followers generally otherwise. It's best not to be dependent on anyone else if possible, but it might not always be possible. You'll have to go with God and figure out what His will for you is individually, as I cannot say.

At that time the state will be hunting down the Church in general though, so relying on others then puts yourself at disadvantage and subject to their loyalties and kindness, which can change in a single moment of anger – and with an Orwellian state using everything to spy, it may only take one misspoken word around things like cellphones and any of the other devices used to treat the populace as the enemies of the state.

At that point, being on social media and using so much technology as we even have now might be a death sentence for many. It probably won't be for a while, maybe not even in my lifetime, but when it is here I have no doubt the state will use everything at hand to quickly hunt everyone down. For myself I will remain online for now, as the few real friends I have are online, but during the tribulation the internet will be a deathtrap for many. Things like how facebook tracks everyone in households and so much of Project LifeLog otherwise will be done still and used to find everyone deemed an enemy. So be careful then.

It might seem impossible to give up addiction to so much easy socialization, though I'd imagine censorship will be far more prevalent and frustrating toward the end and such may help many not to care about sharing their opinions anymore, but it could be the other way too wherein they allow for freedom of speech completely but they hunt down those which say the wrong words and have an AI chatbot mimic them so as to pretend that they're still there. Either way, when it is really the end, such addiction will actually need to be given up. It would probably be best to live as far away from anything with cameras or microphones as possible, if possible then.

Hopefully it will be many years away, but when it's here, do protect yourselves. Get away from all the crap, find places to hide and live off the grid. It's best to learn survival skills before having to live in a survival scenario. Probably better to not have firearms, as you'll be on a list, but if crossbows don't require registration and can be bought with cash it would be best to get those, otherwise learn to build weapons on your own and for friends you trust, not firearms but like bows and other simple ranged weapons for hunting.

The waters will probably be even more poisoned than they are now with so much mercury and strontium, but such poisons take a while to have an effect, so fishing could do for a short term food supply, but it would be best to avoid standing by waters for hours as drones and satellites will be watching those obvious types of locations. Keeping to forests and underground, minimizing time in clearings and in open view of the sky would be best then.

For now such will sound like merely absurd paranoia, but it will be necessary for basic survival in the end. So many things like jobs and struggling to barely survive while surrounded by expensive buildings owned by rich jerks will basically be replaced by struggling to survive but surrounded by nature, so for most at least that's a step up.

Yeah, I know, it doesn't sound like that, and so many bugs will be no fun, but bugs by themselves are mostly just annoying and the more deadly of them just need to be avoided, but the myriad forms of electronic bugs within civilization then will be very deadly for anyone who says the wrong things around them or, if their face is mapped out already, just being seen by a camera. So, it's trade offs either way, but I'd rather put up with actual bugs rather than the electronic variety then.

No matter what, read your Bibles then. My own interpretations could be wrong, read it and interpret it for yourselves and don't let any form of knowledge priests tell you what to think. Think for yourselves, but please never give up and never let anyone convince you to reject Christ or accept the mark. So many things will be traps, and you will need to no longer worry about providing for yourselves in the ways the rich convince the poor that they must, but trust in God and never give up.

IN THE FULLNESS OF TIME

Again: I could be wrong, okay?

This probably will sound like heresy, but so does anything new via cognitive dissonance, so whatever. Here's what I hope might be true anyway. Consider the verse Revelation 12:12,

"Therefore rejoice, ye heavens, and ye that dwell in them. Woe to the inhabiters of the earth and of the sea! for the devil is come down unto you, having great wrath, because he knoweth that he hath but a short time."

Now, translations do vary, and I generally prefer NIV myself, but I like how KJV at least implies the sea will be inhabited along with the earth and of course that would mean inhabited by humans and not merely sea creatures otherwise. But even more awesome might be the first part, if "rejoice ye heavens, and ye that dwell in them" refers to firstly space as the heavens, such as in Psalms 19:1 in which it says "the heavens declare the glory of

God", though if it referred to Heaven and not merely space, that would just be like, well, yay for those already dead. Woo for them. Hopefully it means *the heavens* though and not *Heaven*.

Now, the beginning this segment of chapter 12, verse 7, it is actually is referring to Heaven rather than the heavens, talking about how the archangel Michael kicked the devil out of Heaven, but in the verses leading up to this used the singular form, heaven (and in Greek ουρανω in verses 7, 8, and 10,) but the plural form in verse 12, heavens (ουρανοι). I do not pretend to know Greek, and it could just be like an idiom or something, but there is a difference at least and I hope it might refer to the same "heavens" in verse 12 as it does in Psalm 19:1, although the word used there in the Septuagint is επακουσαι rather than ουρανοι, both are plural at least and I think the prefix there is like epi- which would be like saying "the face of the heavens" probably, but I do not know for sure. The Hebrew used is a plural word too off course, שמים shamayim, which was also used in Genesis 1:1, so there is also a difference between Psalms 19:1 compared to Revelation 12:12, but it is at least plural, heavens, in both places. I cannot say for sure, but I think it probably refers to space rather than Heaven. I could be wrong though, and it could mean nothing much more than Plato's "only the dead have seen the end of war" as lame and sad as that would be, but whatever is truth is truth though regardless of whatever we might want it to be.

Earlier on it talks about the woman giving birth to the Son, and in hypothesis it would refer to Mary and in thesis it would refer to Israel, and in hypothesis Christ' earthly caretakers were hunted by Harod, and in thesis you have the holocaust. So perhaps in a similar manner verse 12 could mean both the "yay for already being dead" meaning as well as, perhaps, some portion of humanity having colonized space. Maybe only some of the solar system, if FTL isn't invented before the end.

I probably sound really crazy, yay, but regardless I would hope that God may allow a fair percentage of humanity to dwell in the Heavens. And by the way, in my work of fiction Fullness Of Time, I wasn't meaning to refer to Michael the archangel by my character Michael the INTJ hermit who would just be plainly human, and I have no idea how it might really play out. Hopefully humanity will live in space though, and I do think an orbital ring is the most probable route to spreading out the fastest, but it wouldn't require internal sabotage to take down. If earth became tyrannical while the nations throughout the solar system were self sufficient, simply firing rail guns at it or redirecting asteroids and exploding them so as to shotgun out the shrapnel would work, but there could be defenses made to deal with micrometeorites and maybe energy shields will be made by then (and so internal sabotage would be the way to go, but I do not know and my story is just a story I hope everyone would like.)

However it may happen though, the last of the

last days will suck for most, and I hope as many people as possible will be living elsewhere other throughout the solar system or however far technologically we may be allowed to travel. The more spread out we are, the more freedom and the more life everywhere, and so, even though only the Earth outright has been given to us according to Genesis, we could still fill as much as possible with life and make all those many waste places into places to dwell. While the tyrannical government of Earth and the rich worship death as they greedily fight over resources, humanity otherwise could still live in abundance elsewhere.

It would probably require the colonies to be able to militarily stand against Earth, but such is the benefit of an orbital ring which can be destroyed and set Earth back, while on Mars massive warships could be built and launched directly from the surface rather than in orbit as would have to be done on Earth.

I do not know how it will play out, I could be wrong, but I truly hope God will allow humanity to have a future in space before the very end.

CORRECTIONS TO CURRENT TECHNOLOGY

Basically: enough with the spyware.

Cellphones and every electronic device ought to have physical power switches rather than just software controlled power modes. As such, unless unplugged and with the battery removed, the devices are never fully off. Enough with that. It's wasteful of power too, though little individually, when billions of people have such devices every little watt adds up. That's needless waste for the sake of convenience and treating everyone like pre-criminals until proven guilty.

Also, there should be physical switches for cameras and microphones on every device that has them too, and fewer devices should have them. Perhaps with LED physically hardwired to each component to indicate when they have power, which would help people remember to turn them off when not being used.

There should also be warm temperature quantum entanglement developed and miniaturized. Migrating birds use quantum coupling I read once, as a means of a compass of sorts, and so somehow they must have either a warm temperature superconductor or some other design for using such effects. I do not know exactly how, but it is possible to do and thus it should be developed and replace microwave technologies with quantum entanglement. That way, it will work regardless of distance instantaneously and will not require irradiation towers nor giving one's location out with the signal either.

SUMMARY: THE UNFAIRNESS OF EVERYTHING

"You will always have the poor among you,..." - John 12:8a

It honestly would be nice if somehow socialism or something like that could work. Except with Christianity rather than atheism as the religion for the nation, unlike in the tyrannies which had so many murders by the evil state. Of course better checks and balances too, and not having rights removed.

Really, with how all the nations spend so much on war, you'd think some of that taxation money could be spent on the percentage of population unable to support themselves, but no, apparently it's somehow "bad" to help the civilians of one's own population while instead using the money which could be spent on the poor upon killing people in other lands, which in this Isaiah 5:20 world is "good" apparently. How stupid. It's "socialism", and thereby "evil", to help the poor with the extortion of taxation upon those able to support themselves, but it's super fine and dandy to use the extortion of taxation upon the military, upon the various 4th amendment violating agencies, upon all the rest of the scams and schemes of the oligarchs in power.

Yes, socialism in many nations and history so far has been bad. Why? No checks and balances. Power is too centralized, too easily corrupted. Even with the American system of checks and balances, it has been corrupted and eroded away over the centuries. Probably every system, no matter what, will eventually be corrupted. No matter what defense you build, someone will find a way to work around it.

For so many though, life really is unfair. Have someone like Bobby Fischer or Magnus Carlsen play a game of chess having only a king on the board, while their opponents have a full set of pieces. No matter however good a player they may be and however crappy their opponent, they will lose. It is impossible. No amount of goading them with "you just need to try harder! Put in more elbow grease and buy more blinker fluid!" is going to do absolutely NOTHING to help. Pretending they're just lazy or stupid for not winning, that is insane. That's just playing into the artificial divide Operation

Mockingbird has set you upon.

You know what's also crazy? Selling know-ledge. Sure, books have prices on them, and authors should be paid for their work (which I of course am slightly biased for since I'm aspiring to be a novelist.) But I don't mean like $20 for a $200 text-book at used book stores, I mean $2,000 per class type insanity. That is absurd. Sure though, you get student loans to "pay" for them, which is just an en-slavement program that you can't get out of. Not for most anyway, and if you do, then you get shamed for tax payers footing your bill. Oh yes, maybe they pay 0.0001 pennies on the dollar or something, IDK. The department of war still takes like 53 cents on the dollar, yet that's "ok". How?

Now, of course student loans are why the cost of college is so high. Colleges are businesses, and they'll take all the money they can get. There is no real limit, except for how much the customer is willing to pay. Who is the customer? The state. What are they buying from college? "Education for the nation"? No, just more debt slaves, indebted to the state, and if unable to pay then, instead of help-ing them find work, they are denied working for the state. That's stupid. Their certifications, which they earned, may be nullified, disabling them from working, which is both evil and stupid. 20 out of 50 states so far also take away driver's licenses, which is yet more insanity, because it cuts them off from being able to find any work they'd need to drive to. How does that make sense if the goal were to be improving the economic situation as a whole?

Of course it doesn't make any sense that way, but how does it? They want a dependent population, having to live in cities, which will all burn if WW3 ever happens. They want the state to be the god of the people, and reliant upon the state for everything. It's a cult, it's a mafia. It's wrong as it is.

Is there a proper place for the state? Yes, via Romans 13 and the rest, it can be made good. Often corrupt leaders throughout history have made every nation under every labeled form of government into a nightmare for many of their populations. Yes, numbers wise, atheistic socialism, in which human life is devalued and made a commodity, has killed the most number of people. Socialism itself is not the problem, but atheism embedded within it, replacing God with the state, that's a major problem, along with no checks and balances. I'm sure there are other problems too, but those are the ones that need the most fixing.

But back to selling knowledge. Should it even be sold? Maybe, but not for absurd prices. There should be no more student loans, only grants. No more debt slavery programs to appeal to ISTJs, that's stupid. Sure, it will cost the state money, thus the taxpayers money, money which is already being paid. Make it so the state will only pay so much and no more, in grants alone, and make student loans illegal (especially loans by the schools themselves, by which they hold your degree ransom.) Colleges will drop their prices immediately. They don't need anywhere near the funding they're getting via extortion currently. Nuke that crap from orbit, metaphorically. Colleges will become affordable overnight.

There should also be a year of Jubilee, which is every 50 years all debts are cancelled. And to solve the problem of people making debt based investments right at the end of the 50 years, you draw lots once each year with it being a 1/50th chance each year, thus it could happen sooner or later, but it's not having the problem of dealing with scammers of that sort.

And there should be no compound interest, just simple interest. No hiding how much things cost with friendly looking numbers hiding exponential debt slavery programs which SJ types will nag you into following because, "it's what I did and it's what everyone should do", despite the "normal" pathways to the American Dream being paved with landmines by so very many legalistic scams and extortionary schemes otherwise.

There should be a proper job placement program too, for those looking for work in which they fit, rather than just telling people "you're on your own! Good luck! Try not to die!" Yeah, no, enough with Darwinism being idolized as "capitalism", that's evil. We're all created equal, we're all made in the image of God and deserve to live, unless anyone commits a capital crime of course, but being unable to find a way in life to be rich is not a capital crime. Everyone should be held up, given proper safety nets, and not have to constantly worry about starving or being homeless.

Oh, but what about the lazy and complacent? The "system surfers"? So what? Let them rest. Are most people really like that? No. Most want nice things, most want luxuries rather than mere subsistence. Yet, the welfare programs as they exist discourage working too much, otherwise they go from being able to survive with state programs to making just barely above the threshold of the programs and yet still nowhere near what they need to survive. It's this flaw in the system which artificially makes those stuck on state programs seem ambitionless, but in truth, I believe, most of them are just trapped within deliberately impossible circumstances. Make it so they don't have stupid limits, and they'll be able to surpass their condition. Give them a basic income, and don't punish them for bettering themselves by finding work that doesn't underpay them.

There really shouldn't be work that underpays either. Sure, you have whining about small businesses that say they're going to go out of business or have to keep short staffed always (which they all do anyway) if they pay their workers like suggested in James 5:1-6 rather than funneling up most of the wealth that the workers earn for the company so as to just make those already rich ever richer. "Oh, but capitalism is god and socialism is the devil!" Oh shut the heck up. This is one thing democrats have right. You know, murdering babies for convenience, that's evil, but paying workers their wages, that's good. If necessary, only require megacorporations to pay living wages while giving more freedom to mom and pop shops. There you go.

Anyway, though we may always have poor, the situation should be improved as much as possible, even if not completely possible, find a way to make things work as good as possible rather than anymore somehow pretending Darwinism is the ideal situation.

It isn't, neither Darwinism nor atheistic communism are right, but that doesn't mean those are the only options. There should be fairness sought for, people should not have to be enslaved by debt and struggle for the basics. Find ways to make things work rather than pretend everything is impossible. If you think everything is perfect now, then may you be shown how wrong you are by being humbled to the level of those you look down upon.

Really now, thank you for reading and feel free to mock and troll me all you like. Take care.

ABOUT THE AUTHOR

Ben Fournier is an autodidactic student of text-books with Asperger's syndrome, former wage slave, INTJ-t/RLOEI, and cares for his silly birds. Sure, if you go after the ethos via ad hominem attacks, you can certainly mock me for being a no-body, but that just shows you don't bother with the logos. Congrats with the inevitable mocking and scoffing, proving out how intelligent you are by going after irrelevant things, I'm sure you can be very proud of yourself attacking the person rather than considering what is said. Cry "heretic" to the religion of Darwinism under the name of "laissez-faire" all you like, I don't care. Both extreme capitalism and atheistic communism are stupid, there need to be better limits against tyranny in all forms. So mock all you like, if that's all you can do, but if you are able, please listen and consider rather than just behave like a parakeet. Not that parakeets aren't cute, but they hardly say anything original. Most don't seem to anyway.

www.ingramcontent.com/pod-product-compliance
Lightning Source LLC
Chambersburg PA
CBHW051231250726
48655CB00006B/2716